DATE DUE

6-1-00

BASKETBALL LEGENDS

Kareem Abdul-Jabbar
Charles Barkley
Larry Bird
Wilt Chamberlain
Clyde Drexler
Julius Erving
Patrick Ewing
Anfernee Hardaway
The Head Coaches
Grant Hill
Juwan Howard
Allen Iverson
Magic Johnson
Michael Jordan
Shawn Kemp
Jason Kidd
Reggie Miller
Alonzo Mourning
Hakeem Olajuwon
Shaquille O'Neal
Gary Payton
Scottie Pippen
David Robinson
Dennis Rodman
John Stockton

CHELSEA HOUSE PUBLISHERS

BASKETBALL LEGENDS

GARY PAYTON

Howard Blatt

Introduction by
Chuck Daly

CHELSEA HOUSE PUBLISHERS
Philadelphia

Produced by Choptank Syndicate, Inc.

Editor and Picture Researcher: Norman L. Macht
Production Coordinator and Editorial Assistant: Mary E. Hull
Design and Production: Lisa Hochstein
Cover Illustrator: Bradford Brown

© 1999 by Chelsea House Publishers,
a division of Main Line Book Co.
Printed and bound in the United States of America.

First Printing

1 3 5 7 9 8 6 4 2

Library of Congress Cataloging-in-Publication Data

Blatt, Howard.
        Gary Payton / by Howard Blatt.
          p.   cm. — (Basketball legends)
        Includes bibliographical references (p.   ) and index.
        Summary: A biography of the tough-talking point guard
for the Seattle Sonics who was named the NBA Defensive Player
of the Year in 1996.
        ISBN 0-7910-4578-1 (hardcover)
        1. Payton, Gary, 1968-   — Juvenile literature. 2. Basketball
players—United States—Biography—Juvenile literature. 3. Seattle
SuperSonics (Basketball team)—Juvenile literature. [1. Payton,
Gary, 1968- . 2. Afro-American basketball players. 3. Basketball
players. 4. Afro-Americans—Biography.] I. Title. II. Series.
GV884.P39B63 1998
796.323'092—dc21
[B]   97-46623
                                                           CIP
                                                            AC

CONTENTS

BECOMING A
BASKETBALL LEGEND

Chuck Daly

What does it take to be a basketball superstar? Two of the three things it takes are easy to spot. Any great athlete must have excellent skills and tremendous dedication. The third quality needed is much harder to define, or even put in words. Others call it leadership or desire to win, but I'm not sure that explains it fully. This third quality relates to the athlete's thinking process, a certain mentality and work ethic. One can coach athletic skills, and while few superstars need outside influence to help keep them dedicated, it is possible for a coach to offer some well-timed words in order to keep that athlete fully motivated. But a coach can do no more than appeal to a player's will to win; how much that player is then capable of ensuring victory is up to his own internal workings.

In recent times, we have been fortunate to have seen some of the best to play the game. Larry Bird, Magic Johnson, and Michael Jordan had all three components of superstardom in full measure. They brought their teams to numerous championships, and made the players around them better. (They also made their coaches look smart.)

I myself coached a player who belongs in that class, Isiah Thomas, who helped lead the Detroit Pistons to consecutive NBA crowns. Isiah is not tall—he's just over six feet—but he could do whatever he wanted with the ball. And what he wanted to do most was lead and win.

All the players I mentioned above and those whom this series will chronicle are tremendously gifted athletes, but for the most part, you can't play professional basketball at all unless you have excellent skills. And few players get to stay on their team unless they are willing to dedicate themselves to improving their talents even more, learning about their opponents, and finding a way to join with their teammates and win.

It's that third element that separates the good player from the superstar, the memorable players from the legends of the game. Superstars know when to take over the game. If the situation calls for a defensive stop, the superstars stand up and do it. If the situation calls for a key pass, they make it. And if the situation calls for a big shot, they want the ball. They don't want the ball simply because of their own glory or ego. Instead they know—and their teammates know—that they are the ones who can deliver, regardless of the pressure.

The words "legend" and "superstar" are often tossed around without real meaning. Taking a hard look at some of those who truly can be classified as "legends" can provide insight into the things that brought them to that level. All of them developed their legacy over numerous seasons of play, even if certain games will always stand out in the memories of those who saw them. Those games typically featured amazing feats of all-around play. No matter how great the fans thought the superstars were, these players were capable of surprising the fans, their opponents, and occasionally even themselves. The desire to win took over, and with their dedication and athletic skills already in place, they were capable of the most astonishing achievements.

CHUCK DALY, now the head coach of the Orlando Magic, guided the Detroit Pistons to two straight NBA championships, in 1989 and 1990. He earned a gold medal as coach of the 1992 U.S. Olympic basketball team—the so-called "Dream Team"—and was inducted into the Pro Basketball Hall of Fame in 1994.

1

MEASURING UP TO MICHAEL

Two he Seattle SuperSonics had climbed through the rugged Western Conference to reach the 1996 National Basketball Association Finals, knocking off the Sacramento Kings, the defending champion Houston Rockets, and the tough Utah Jazz.

Then, with the world watching in the Finals, the powerful Chicago Bulls beat the Sonics three straight times, intimidating them out of their usual take-no-prisoners, in-your-face style. One more loss to the Chicago Bulls and the Sonics would be branded once again as lacking the heart and character of a true championship contender.

That had been the popular bottom line on the Sonics each of the two previous seasons, when they had averaged 60 wins per campaign, only to be eliminated from the playoffs in first-round upsets by the Denver Nuggets and the Los Angeles Lakers. Like their combative court leader, Gary Payton, whose failures and erratic behavior

Gary Payton vents his frustration at an official during the first quarter of a playoff game against the Chicago Bulls in June of 1996.

during these playoffs were fatal for Seattle, the Sonics were dismissed as too high-strung, too immature, too unpredictable.

Feeling more than his share of the heat again was Payton, the superstar point guard so instrumental in the Sonics' greatest successes and most galling failures. He had enjoyed another All-Star season in which he was hailed as the league's top defender. He had led the league in steals and had proven himself to be a more under-control leader. However, Payton found himself in over his head against the swarming Bulls. Phil Jackson's remarkable defensive team focused on forcing Gary to give up the ball, reducing the ultra-aggressive Payton to a tentative, non-impact performer.

In Game 1, Payton's trash-talking encounter with Michael Jordan was typical of the cocky chatter that had angered opponents and fueled Gary's competitive fires beginning in his school-yard days in Oakland. But, on this night, the tongue-flapping was perhaps the only evidence that the Sonics' No. 20 really was Payton, as, for once, his game lacked the same bite as his mouth.

On the occasions he wasn't being hounded by two defenders into giving up the ball, the 6' 4" Payton found he could not take the 6' 6" Ron Harper inside the lane and shoot over him the way he had done with smaller opponents in previous rounds. Payton missed his first six shots, didn't score until the second quarter, and wound up with a 13-point, 6-for-17 shooting performance and six assists in a 107–90 defeat. Even his turnovers were of the passive variety.

On defense, Seattle coach George Karl kept Payton away from Michael Jordan, fearing foul trouble or fatigue would take a toll on the Sonics' lone healthy ballhandler.

On the off-day before Game 2, Sonics scout Brendan Malone begged Payton to unleash more of the swagger that defined his usual demeanor, telling him about the caged-animal intensity that Isiah Thomas brought to the Finals while leading the Detroit Pistons to two championships. Thus inspired, Gary engaged Jordan in several verbal confrontations in Game 2. But, again, Payton's production didn't keep up with his mouth. He managed only 13 points and three assists—eight points and two assists below his averages through the first three rounds of the playoffs.

There didn't seem to be much more for the clench-jawed Payton to say after Jordan scored 27 first-half points and 36 overall in a Game 3 rout on Seattle's home court that left the Sonics a defeat away from another summer of defending themselves. Most of Payton's 19 points and nine assists in that game came after Jordan had put the game away.

"They have guys like [Scottie] Pippen and Jordan and [Dennis] Rodman, guys who have won championships coming in playing guys like myself who are here for the first time," said the humbled Payton.

With the Sonics having lost a season-high three straight, and the Bulls riding a nine-game post-season winning streak and a 14–1 playoff record, it seemed like a good time for drastic measures, new strategies, and a few gambles. So Payton approached his coach on the day before Game 4 and asked to be a designated stopper on Jordan, the eight-time NBA scoring champ.

Karl had said before the series, "I thought when I came here four years ago, when Jordan was playing, Gary was the only guy who had any guts to play him. Everybody else was in awe of him . . . Gary has always challenged him. Gary has never backed off of him mentally."

In fact, Payton was eager.

"I just told coach if we have to go that route where I have to get a couple of minutes, 20 to 25 minutes on him to help him out, then we'll have to go that route," said Payton.

Knowing his team would be buoyed in the backcourt by the return of the sore-backed Nate McMillan, Karl finally permitted Payton, the NBA's Defensive Player of the Year—nicknamed "The Glove" for his ability to cling so tightly—to guard the game's greatest scorer for significant minutes. Before the Sonics went out onto the floor for Game 4 on June 12, Karl told his emotional team to be its wildly aggressive self for the first time all series.

When the game began, with the 17,072 at Key Arena uncertain if they were on hand to witness a burial or a revival, the Bulls were smelling blood and looking to deliver a disabling early blow.

Only 1:40 into the contest, Jordan backed in against the smaller Payton, then whirled and hit an 11-foot jumper for the game's first points.

Not a soul could have guessed that this basket would be Jordan's final field goal of the entire quarter.

When Payton's alley-oop pass produced a Shawn Kemp dunk—the trademark collaboration of the stylish Payton and the power forward—the game was tied and there was a hint of what was to come.

After the Bulls had jumped out to a 6–2 lead, Payton took a kick-out pass from Kemp and nailed a 23-foot jumper from three-point range.

This time, there was no hint of hesitation in pulling the trigger. The lost soul who had missed nine of his 10 three-point attempts over the first three games of the Finals was gone. In his place was the coldblooded assassin of a jump shooter who made 32 percent of his threes during the season and 40 percent of his shots from downtown over the first three rounds of playoffs.

Payton's trifecta ignited a sudden 13–2 run for Seattle as the Sonics, having rediscovered their defensive presence behind the Jordan-containing efforts of Payton, held the Bulls without a basket for five minutes. Payton found Kemp for a layup and later nailed another three, this time from 25 feet away, on a pass from Hersey Hawkins, for a 13–8 Sonic advantage.

Chicago Bulls guard Michael Jordan holds the ball just out of Gary Payton's reach during Game 4 of the NBA Finals, June 12, 1996, in Seattle.

Finally freed to roam by the insertion of McMillan into the lineup, Payton took McMillan's pass over Steve Kerr's head on the drive for a pick-and-roll layup and a 25–19 Seattle lead with 36.3 seconds left.

"The reason I got back to my game is that Nate was at the point a little bit. He got me into a lot of picks and I got to move off [away from] the ball," said the slippery Payton. "I could put Michael on the baseline and he had to guard me off curls, picks, and stuff like that. When I can get free like that, I think my game is a little more loose."

"Payton came out and got going very quickly and he received some confidence," said Jordan. "And then, when Nate McMillan came in, they worked the two-man game very well with Gary coming off the screen."

By quarter's end, Payton had eight points, three assists, and one steal, Jordan had only three points on just three field-goal attempts, and the Sonics led, 25–21. Payton, one of the few players with the quickness and the moxie to successfully deny Jordan the basketball, was doing just that.

Gary and the Sonics were just getting started. The Sonics scored the first 11 points of the second quarter. Another Payton layup, off another pass from McMillan, followed a Jordan turnover. Payton nailed another three-point jumper on a pass from Sam Perkins to make it 34–21 with 2:07 gone in the period. After Payton located McMillan with a set-up pass for a three, the Sonics were sitting atop a commanding 39–25 margin.

Jordan finally shook free to retaliate with an 18-foot jumper, but Payton found Kemp for a 20-footer. With the Bulls in a 43–27 hole, it was Michael who wore his frustration on his face and tongue. Jordan was called for an offensive foul and his histrionics led to a technical—rarely called on His Airness out of deference to his stature. The boiling over was a tipoff that Payton and the Sonics had taken Michael so far out of his game, he no longer felt he could impose his iron will on the outcome.

By halftime, Payton had 13 points on 5-for-10 shooting from the floor to go with six assists, while Jordan had only seven points on 3-for-9 shooting and three turnovers. The Sonics led, 53–32, at the break. The stunned Bulls found themselves on ice, along with the bottles of champagne that would remain unopened on this night. With an 11-point second quarter, Chicago had tied the record for the fewest points scored in a quarter of an NBA Finals game. And the Bulls' 32 first-half points tied a franchise playoff low, two shy of an NBA Finals record.

Payton made certain the Bulls didn't claw their way back into it, opening the second-half scoring with a driving layup and gliding in off another to keep the Sonics' lead at a comfortable 59–43. Another Payton-to-Kemp pass for a slam at 6:06 put the Sonics up 66–45. A Perkins jam, off a Payton feed in the closing seconds of the third

A determined Payton passes his rival, Michael Jordan, in the third quarter of the NBA Sonics/Bulls finals. The Bulls won the series' final game.

quarter, pushed Seattle into an 84–63 lead and the Bulls never came closer than 19 after that.

Payton was brilliant, finishing with 21 points on 7-for-15 shooting, including 3-of-6 on three-point attempts, plus 11 assists and two steals. The Sonics—who came in averaging 88 points per game on 42 percent accuracy over the first three games—converted an astounding 56.2 percent of the shots from the floor, compared to the Bulls' 40 percent mark. The 107–86 final margin marked only the second time all season that Chicago had lost by more than 10 points.

Jordan finished with 23 points, but they came on 6-for-19 shooting. Figure in his four turnovers and two assists, his flagrant foul, his technical foul, and his double-dribble violation, and it added up to what may have been Michael's worst performance in 11 postseasons and 137 playoff games.

"I was frustrated, but I think we all were," said Jordan, who had averaged 31 points per game over the first three games against Seattle. "It seemed like nothing went right for us . . . Their defense is very active and you've got to give them that credit. But a lot of it had to do with the way we played in the game . . . I didn't shoot the ball well. None of us shot the ball well."

But in Game 4 and again in Game 6, when Jordan could not find the range in the Bulls' series-clinching win, Payton appeared to have plenty to do with applying the brakes on Michael. Jordan shot only 37 percent over the last three games of the Finals.

"I tried to make him work on the defensive end and offensive end, get him a little tired and whatever happens, happens," said Payton about Jordan after Game 4. "Tonight, I was a little more aggressive. I couldn't just stand here and let him rest. I had to go at him a little more and I did . . . He was taking shots he doesn't normally take."

"Shawn and Gary gave us big, manly stuff," said Karl. "Defensively, Gary was very good."

"Gary played his game," said Kemp. "That is his game to get up and play good defense. To come on the offensive end and be aggressive. His defense was premium tonight. That is probably what won the game for us."

"He is not the Defensive Player of the Year for nothing," said Hawkins.

The Sonics, now bristling with the energy and confidence to force the series back to Chicago with a Game 5 victory, were nobody's chumps— and Payton could no longer be dismissed as the volcanic talent who always led them nowhere.

"We were so scared we didn't do anything right for the first three games," said Payton. "But once we realized we had nothing to lose, the fear disappeared . . . It meant everything—pride especially. It showed we had some guts, some character. Once we stopped being scared and started to play our kind of basketball, it got to the point where the Bulls were scared of us. The last thing they wanted was to play us in Game 7."

Certainly, Payton sent a nonverbal message to Jordan that Michael would not forget if they met again with a title on the line: You can be stopped, and the next time the real Gary Payton won't take so long to surface.

"One of the mistakes I made was not putting Gary straight nose-to-nose with Michael [from the start and for longer stretches]," admitted Karl. "Putting our heart against their heart."

2

MEAN AL
AND SURVIVING
OAKTOWN

When NBA star Gary Payton went home to the mean streets of East Oakland, to a neighborhood overcome by drugs and crime, he was instantly recognized and idolized as the living proof that there were ways out of those grim streets for anyone blessed with the talent, determination, and firm guiding hand that enabled Payton to make his basketball dreams come true.

Gary Dwayne Payton was born June 23, 1968, in Oakland. The youngest of the five children of Annie and Alfred Owen Payton, he grew up in the same neighborhood as his oldest brother Greg and Alfred, the sibling closest in age to Gary. But the streets were much more treacherous by the time impressionable Gary was walking them.

During his childhood, Gary strained to keep the lowest of profiles, hoping the local drug dealers would leave him alone. Many of his friends were active in gangs, including one

With his parents' help, Gary Payton graduated from high school in Oaktown, California, and went on to play for Oregon State University.

long-time companion and frequent visitor to the Payton home, a boy known by the street name of Little D. Little D never tried to recruit his buddy into the High Street Bank Boys gang. Little D went to prison on a drug dealing conviction while Gary became a pro basketball star, but their friendship survived.

Gary has remained close to many of his childhood running mates and helped at least one to escape the neighborhood. Milton Jackson, another Payton friend from their days as five-year-olds on the Jefferson Elementary playground, stopped playing ball when he broke his leg and eventually succumbed to the drug life. Payton used his National Basketball Association riches to give Jackson the gift of a college education at Seattle University, in exchange for the single promise that his street-running days were over.

Payton understood that he was not so different from the kids who were overcome by the temptation of the drug life, that he could have been one of them if not for his athletic gifts and the determination of his dad, Big Al.

The old-fashioned Southern values taught to Al by the great-aunt who had raised him in Mississippi made him both a no-nonsense taskmaster and a dedicated provider for his family. Al worked a shift as a chef at one restaurant in the mornings, worked at another in the evenings, and occasionally labored at a local cannery so Gary would have enough money for new sneakers.

"Money changes people's minds," said Al. "I made sure Gary never had to sell drugs to get any."

"Gary was the baby and Al put a lot of time and effort into him," said Annie. "And Gary always listens to him. Whatever Al says, Gary will do."

Al had little Gary carry the balls to the playground for himself and Greg. He steadfastly kept his youngest son focused on the game they both loved. Al had been a shooting guard at Alcorn A&M. He had a physical style and an appetite for competition. The kids he coached in the Oakland Neighborhood Basketball League called him "Mr. Mean"—a tag he wore proudly on the license plate of his Nissan 280Z.

"I taught the kid the look, the intimidation, the meanness," said Al. "When I played, I liked to hurt people."

The lessons Al taught Gary on the court were often the painful kind, but Gary came to understand that in basketball, as in life, nobody gives you anything.

"He wouldn't let me win," remembered Gary.

"Gary was so little. I told him, 'No matter what your size, be a man,'" said Al.

Eventually, as a 10th grader, the son began dominating their one-on-one wars.

Among the lessons that Gary learned from his father and from those tough streets was to never back down, to always talk the talk, and to always back it up in a big way.

Gary's trash-talking had its roots in the nighttime games involving kids and adults at Jefferson gym.

When the nasty talk from opponents reduced little Gary to tears, Al would say to his son and teammate, "Don't worry. Daddy will get them."

And then he would make good on his promise.

"In Oakland, you have to talk trash or you will be had," said Al. "Oakland is a tough town. Everybody wants to . . . have their way. If you don't fight back, you will get whipped every day. You don't have to win, but people have to know that you're always ready to go if that is what it takes."

Gary's sister Sharon was an accomplished trash-talking softball player. Greg, a high school basketball star who played two seasons for San Francisco State, and Alfred also ran their mouths on the court. Gary would interrupt his own one-man clinics in scoring, stealing, and assisting to infuriate opponents by screaming at their bench, "Get somebody out here who can guard me."

"I talk to my opponent, so he makes it a personal thing," said Gary. "He starts playing me one-on-one and forgets about his team. Meanwhile, I am still playing team ball and eating him up. Some guys try talking back, but you can't get a talker when a talker is talking to you."

Of course, you can't talk unless you can play. As his coach, Al drummed into Gary's head the importance of defense and passing. If those aspects of his game faltered, Al would keep Gary on the bench for extended periods in those Oakland Neighborhood Basketball League contests.

"I know he loved to play, so if he did something wrong, I sat him down," said Al. "Once he went back in, he would take it out on his opponents."

Al wanted his son to attend Skyline High School, which was in a prosperous, mostly white neighborhood, but Gary wanted to follow his friends to nearby Fremont High. Shortly before it was time for him to enroll, a youngster was stabbed to death in a fight on the Fremont playground, and Gary accepted his parents' request that he attend Skyline.

Skyline had never won a title in the tough Oakland Athletic League. Al's theory was that the white players were scared to beat the mostly black powerhouses like Fremont because of what might happen after the game. Because of the threat of violence, games were played in the afternoons, often under the vigilance of Oakland police. Taunting talk between neighborhood rivals often led to physical confrontations, and Al and Alfred were concerned enough to escort Gary to and from each Skyline game.

"You talk about rowdy," said Payton. "The players were on you. The refs were on you. The fans were on you. You had to talk back or you were a sissy. You would get run out of the league. Afterwards, it was a struggle to get out of the gym. Cops had to be everywhere."

Forever yapping at his old neighborhood buddies about how he would embarrass them, Payton beat bitter rival Fremont with a last-second shot in his senior year and the postgame verbal exchange nearly escalated into a riot.

Before proving his mettle on the court, Payton almost let a casual attitude toward his

George Gervin was Payton's favorite basketball player. Here Gervin attempts a basket for the Chicago Bulls, while the 76ers' Julius Erving (left) and Charles Barkley (right) prepare to cover it.

classwork ruin him at Skyline. As a sophomore, Gary's poor grades and bad attitude got him suspended from the team for half a season.

For about two months, Al went to Skyline three times a week because of Gary's misbehavior. Then a teacher called Mr. Mean at home. Al Payton came into his son's math class the next day and humiliated Gary in front of his classmates.

"Because he was a basketball player, he didn't think he had to do anything else," said Al. "I went in there and said to his classmates, 'I am going to show you all he is not a little man, he's a little baby.' And I kind of spanked him in front of everyone. That was that."

Al's effort to drive home his point was aided by Gary's growing realization that the NCAA had passed minimum academic requirements for its student-athletes. His continued refusal to study could imperil his collegiate basketball career.

"He was so cocky, you wanted to kick him in the butt," remembered his Skyline coach, Fred Noel. "But I learned he will do anything necessary to play basketball."

Gary's grades and his attitude improved and he led Skyline to a combined 39–12 record and two OAL titles during his junior and senior years. As a junior, Gary scored 18.3 points per game and had 269 assists in 26 games, carrying the school to a 19–7 season that ended with a loss in the Northern California championship game. In his senior year, Payton averaged 20.6 points on 52.8 percent shooting from the floor, 6.9 rebounds, and 10.5 assists. He was East Bay Player of the Year and an all-state pick as Skyline finished 20–5 and made the second round of the regionals in 1985–86. The school later retired his No. 20.

"In high school, I was offensive-minded," admitted Gary. "I liked George Gervin a lot and you know he didn't play no 'D'."

The recruiters had their doubts, wondering if Payton would turn out to be more trouble than he was worth. Gary had a flamboyant appearance that turned off some coaches at first sight. He wore a diamond earring, which was not commonplace in those days, and had scissor-inscribed into his hair his initials, dollar signs, a champagne glass, and even the floor plan for his dream house.

However, St. John's coach Lou Carnesecca saw Payton play and was impressed. In fact, Gary was set to go to St. John's and was dressed in Redmen's warmups, waiting to announce his choice at a Skyline press conference. But Carnesecca later told him that St. John's had decided to give the scholarship to another player. St. John's was not interested in him after all.

"Gary was devastated, but it made him a better ballplayer," said Al. "He wanted to prove Carnesecca made a mistake. Gary just kept getting better and better, hoping he would get a chance to play St. John's."

Gary had received offers from New Mexico State, North Carolina State, Oregon State, and Stanford. Annie Payton wanted her son go to Oregon State, because assistant coach Jim Anderson talked about Gary becoming the first Payton to get a degree. Al liked Beavers' coach Ralph Miller, who left the Payton house one day with the words, "I'm not calling you anymore. If you want to come, you call me. If you don't call, Oregon State will go on."

Eager to leave the mean streets of Oakland, Gary chose to go north to the quiet timberlands of Corvallis, Oregon.

3

THE GLOVE IS BORN AT OSU

Gary Payton's attitude toward his basketball skills had been shaken by the St. John's rejection; it was a more humble Payton who arrived in Corvallis.

"I was really scared when I went to Oregon State," Gary remembered. "I wasn't sure I could play on the college level. Losing the scholarship to St. John's put ideas like that in my head. I began to think nobody wanted me . . ."

The fear disappeared fast, according to coach Ralph Miller. Gary was highly motivated to prove that Miller's belief in him wasn't misplaced faith.

"He may have walked in a little questioning, but after the first week, he was sure he could play," said the coach. "From the first time he walked on the floor, it was clear that he had talent."

Miller insisted Payton lose the billboard haircut, but the coach allowed Gary to keep his single earring, like the one worn by his dad. And Miller

Oregon State guard Gary Payton looks for a way out and scrambles on the floor as Arizona State players surround him during a 1990 game.

made it clear to Payton from the beginning that a lackadaisical attempt at playing defense would mean no playing time. It was something that Payton needed to hear to get his thinking straight.

"I thought if I would get 40, 50 points a night I would go to the pros and be the greatest scorer in history," said Payton. "But, all of a sudden, coach Miller says, 'You are going to have to play defense to play in my program.'"

Before long, something dawned on the player with the lightning hands and the jackrabbit feet. Payton realized that, with his tools, he could exert the same impact by disrupting teams on the defensive end as he did ruining opponents with his drives to the basket. He became Pac-10 Defensive Player of the Year as a freshman in 1986–87 and had five steals in a game twice, against Gonzaga and Washington.

His ballhandling and distribution skills didn't suffer, either. Gary wasted no time in shattering the Oregon State single-season assist mark held by Freddie Boyd (185 in 1972) with 229. It guaranteed that Boyd, a former pro who was an OSU assistant under Miller, would be the target of plenty of good-natured abuse from Payton.

"If I had been around 20 years ago, you would never have had any records," teased Gary. "You don't want to play me. They would have to have an ambulance stand by to take one of us away. And you know it wouldn't be me."

Payton had six double-figure assist games as a freshman. Gary averaged 7.6 assists, the most by a freshman in NCAA play since assists began to be officially kept on a national basis in 1982. Payton began looking for his shot late in the season, after the Beavers faltered, and he scored in double figures in 22 of 30 games. The game after pulling down a career-high 12 rebounds in a win over Oregon, he rang up a personal-best 20 points in a loss to Arizona.

Even with the improvements in his game, Payton remained a loose cannon, the kind of enemy folks love to hate. As a freshman, he hit a male Oregon cheerleader with a wad of gum after being repeatedly called a "Hookhead."

"My freshman year, I exploded at anything," said Payton. "A referee would call a foul and I would be on him. And the other players, too. As a freshman, I would get into it with the players."

Miller gave him lots of room to be Gary Payton.

"You couldn't take away the kid's style. His cockiness is what makes him tick," said Miller. "Gary also never looks like he is paying attention. But he is. He has the best eyes and ears I've ever known. I never had to tell him anything twice."

Payton was disappointed when an irregular heartbeat prevented him from participating in the United States Olympic trials. He finished his sophomore season on a roll, though, with nine straight double-figure scoring games that included a 30-point explosion against Oregon. In that game, Gary nailed his last 10 field-goal attempts and 14 of 22 overall. Factor in his five assists and he had a hand in 40 of Oregon State's 59 points.

That remarkable effort capped a three-game tear that saw Payton shoot 68.4 percent from the floor, including 9 for 12 from three-point range, and amass 20 assists and eight steals. Gary was an honorable mention All-American, an All-Pac 10 choice, and a member of the United States Basketball Writers Association District 8 All-District team as he led the conference with an average of 7.4 assists and 2.4 steals. He even broke his own school mark for assists with 230.

Before Gary, Oregon State had never been blessed with this kind of playmaking force. Payton was still a junior when he notched 14 assists against St. Joseph's to unseat George Tucker (525) for the top spot on the Beavers' career list. In 1988–89, Gary led his team in scoring (21.8 points per game), assists (8.1), steals (3.0), and minutes (38.0), and ranked second in blocked shots (0.6) and rebounds (4.1). He led the Pac-10 in scoring, assists, and steals in conference games.

Payton had a school-record seven steals plus 20 points, nine assists, and seven rebounds in an 82–69 victory over UCLA. He scored all nine of OSU's overtime points in a 69–64 win at California. Gary bounced back from a bout with the stomach flu for a 41-point, seven-assist,

USC's Dave Wiltz tries to block a pass by OSU's Gary Payton. OSU won the 1988 game, 80–77.

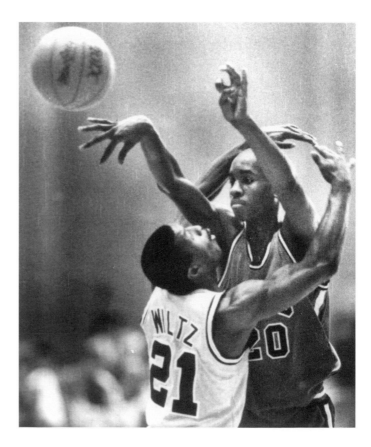

four-steal outburst against Washington State, becoming the first guard to score more than 40 points in a Pac-10 game since 1971.

Gary scored in double figures in the last 24 games of the season and in 28 of 30 overall, earning All-Pac 10 and first-team National Association of Basketball Coaches District 14 All-Star honors. Oregon State was eliminated by Evansville in the first round of NCAA tournament, but not because Payton failed to respond to the occasion. He had 31 points and 10 assists.

"There really isn't anything he can't do," said Miller. "He's probably the quickest player I ever coached. He's an excellent passer, plays excellent defense, and he's unselfish."

And now he had a decision to make: spend his senior year in sleepy Corvallis or jump to the NBA a year early. He opted to remain a Beaver for his fourth and final year of eligibility.

"Staying in school gave me a chance to mature," he said, looking back at his decision later. "I don't think I was ready for the NBA."

He never had cause to regret his choice. Jim Anderson, who had recruited Gary and was now the head coach, told Payton he wanted more points from him in 1989–90. Anderson didn't have to ask twice; Payton removed any doubts that he could be a scorer, defender, and playmaker.

Aided by adjustments to his shooting release, Gary seemed to hit every shot the Beavers needed. As a senior, he averaged 32.6 points per game over an eight-contest stretch from December 10 through January 5.

He beat Tennessee in overtime with a 39-point effort in which he shot 17-of-26 from the floor (including four threes) and amassed nine assists, three steals, and five rebounds. Then Payton tied the single-game Oregon State scoring mark of 48, against Loyola-Marymount on December 19.

During a 35-point, 12-assist dismantling of Louisiana Tech, Payton was nailed with his fourth personal foul with 6:16 left, but he scored eight of the Beavers' last 10 points, including the game-winning jumper with nine seconds left. When Gary got hit with his fourth foul with 4:16 left against Oregon, he scored the next 10 points en route to 30 points and 13 assists in another narrow victory. Finally, Payton shrugged off a fourth foul with 7:11 remaining versus Stanford and scored 10 in the rest of the second half and the overtime for 36 points in a one-point victory.

"The thing I like is that, late in the game, he's not just a good player. He is a great player," said Los Angeles Lakers GM Jerry West.

"Gary has no peers," said Washington coach Lynn Nance. "He is a consummate winner . . . There aren't many like that . . . [just] Magic Johnson and Larry Bird."

Oregon coach Don Monson, against whose team Payton continually scored, said, "It's almost to the point you'd rather have another guy shooting wide open than have Payton shooting with three guys on him."

"When it comes to crunch time, there is no player in America who can get it done better," said Anderson.

Payton enjoyed perhaps his greatest collegiate performance against Southern California on February 22, as he brought his team from a 22-point deficit to a 98–94 overtime victory while shattering the single-game scoring records for OSU and Gill Coliseum. Gary rang up 58 points— the second-highest single-game output in

Pac-10 history—as he made 15 of 20 shots in the second half and the overtime.

"I think that was one of the greatest one-man performances in the history of college basketball," said USC coach George Raveling. "The only thing you do is guard him and pray."

"If Gary Payton is not the best guard in the nation, I don't know who is," said UCLA forward Don McLean.

That night Payton surpassed Steve Johnson's 2,035 as the school's all-time point producer en route to a final total of 2,172, which ranked Payton sixth in Pac-10 annals. Gary averaged 25.7 points, 8.1 assists, and 4.7 rebounds as a senior, shooting 50.4 percent from the floor. He was named College Player of the Year by *Sports Illustrated*, Pac 10 Player of the Year by the conference coaches, and was a first-team pick on the UPI, NABC, and the *Sporting News* All-American squads.

"He is the ultimate complete player," said Anderson. "He makes every player around him better."

Payton finished as the Pac-10 career leader in steals (315) and assists (930) and in second place on the NCAA career list in both categories. The kid with the alleged attitude problem started every game in his four years at OSU.

"He is like a bounty hunter," said Washington State coach Kelvin Sampson. "But I think he gets more respect than any player in the league."

"I just brought my playground game to college and nobody else did," said Payton, explaining his passion for trash talk.

Now it was time to bring it to the pros. The Seattle SuperSonics, intrigued by a player who NBA Director of Scouting Marty Blake said "comes along once in 10 years," made him the second pick in the 1990 draft.

4

LEARNING THE ROPES

Gary Payton was the Sonics' starting point guard from the day that he walked into training camp in the fall of 1990.

Most rookies learn the vast difference between the college game and the pros during a gradual exposure that allows them to commit their mistakes in a more forgiving atmosphere. But Payton's status and $2.7-million-per-year salary insured that he would endure a trial by fire under an immediate spotlight as people rushed to judgment about his skills and his inadequacies.

Payton's one-on-one defense, penetration, finishing skills, fearless manner going to the basket, and speed in the open court, all suggested stardom. But his inability to nail his outside shot in his early seasons as a pro put a cloud over his future in some people's minds.

A dejected Gary Payton sits on the bench during the final moments of a May 7, 1994, playoff game against the Denver Nuggets. Denver beat Seattle 98–84 and won the best-of-five series 3–2.

As a rookie, Payton averaged only 7.2 points per game, an anemic figure for such an accomplished collegiate scorer. He shot just 45 percent from the floor and 7.7 percent from the three-point territory. The scoring difficulties tended to overshadow his averages of 6.4 assists and 2.0 steals, totals which ranked in the league's top 20 in each category.

Later, when Payton looked back on his first year as a pro, he described himself as a victim of self-doubt. But he insisted this was the result of coach K. C. Jones's lack of faith in him.

"I knew what the problem was. It was coaching," insisted Payton. "I couldn't adjust to K. C. Jones's style of coaching. I could not walk the ball up court like he demanded. I wanted to run, and then if I shot the ball and missed, I would get jerked. And that killed my confidence. I got to the point where I didn't like basketball and I didn't want to be here."

Gary's second season, 1991–92, was only slightly better. Payton shot 45.1 percent from the field for a scoring average of 9.4. Payton did join Michael Jordan, Scottie Pippen, and David Robinson as the only NBA players to register more than one triple-double—which means double figures in three statistical categories in one game. Payton amassed 17 points, 11 rebounds, and 12 assists against Golden State and registered 15 points, 10 rebounds, and 13 assists against Utah. But Payton's scoring woes made him the subject of trade rumors.

On January 23, Gary's Seattle career reached a turning point when George Karl replaced Jones as the Sonics' coach. Karl, a feisty former point guard himself, prized defense and saw Payton as a key to his plans of pressing and playing an up-tempo game. He made Gary's development into an offensive and defensive quarterback his top priority. After the coaching change was made, assistant coach Tim Grgurich took Gary aside and showed him films of his scoring explosions in college. "Look at that," he said, "Play like that for us."

Payton lifted his game a notch and the Sonics, who had gone 20–20 under Jones, finished the 1991–92 season at 47–35. They won their first-round playoff against Golden State before falling to Utah in the Western Conference semifinals.

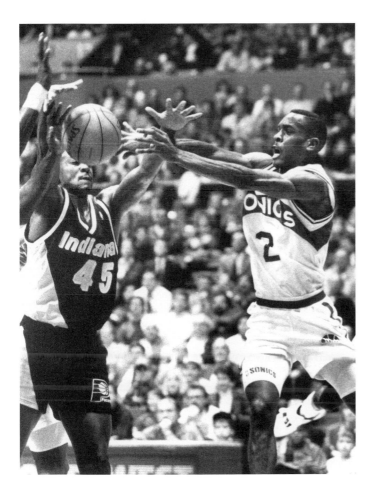

Too many arms go for the ball as Gary Payton's pass fails to make it past the Indiana Pacers guards during a Sonics 1990 home game in Seattle.

The volatile relationship between Karl and Payton, two tough guys who needed each other, began to take shape.

In practice games, Karl deplored the chilly way in which Payton would mock a rookie teammate, make up with him, and then crush him verbally again.

"It is wrong how sometimes he abuses young players," said Karl. "He laughs at them, insults them a little bit . . . He will score 15 in a quarter and every time he scores on them, he will laugh at them. He will say, 'Why are you out here? You don't belong in the league. You are a CBA guy.' He trashes them pretty good . . . To me that is not necessary . . . If he and I played on the same team, we would have a fight in practice every day."

Karl saw a lot of his own sometimes self-destructive rebelliousness in Payton, who tested coaches' patience with his lackadaisical approach to practices and his chronic lateness. But Karl hoped that Gary would relate to him in the more

Larry Bird of the Boston Celtics takes the ball from Gary Payton during a 1991 game in Seattle.

respectful manner that Karl had assumed toward his college coach, the North Carolina legend Dean Smith, many years earlier. It didn't happen.

"When coach Karl came here, his ego was as big as mine," said Payton. "He didn't know how to deal with a player like me, a player who would always talk back to him. We were always griping. I didn't want to cooperate with him and he wanted to control me. I wanted to just go out and play. I didn't want to disrespect him by shouting at him in front of 38,000 people like he was doing to me. I told him, "If you want to tell me something, let's go behind closed doors and do it. Don't embarrass me in front of my teammates and fans."

"I am closer to Gary Payton's mother, girlfriend, and his kids than anybody on this team," said Karl. "But I'll tell you, one time [in a bathroom meeting during halftime at a December 1993 game], my wife [Cathy] asked Gary's daughter if she'd like it if we came to see her at her house in the offseason. And little Racquel said, 'No. Coach can't come into our house. Daddy doesn't want him there.'"

However, on the court, Payton and Karl needed each other. And, with the help of assistant coach Grgurich acting as mediator, Payton and Karl were often brought into the same room to curse each other, just to clear the air. Grgurich had to repeatedly remind the emotional Karl that Payton was too vital to the coach's scheme to be traded. Finally, the hardheaded coach found ways to accommodate his difficult star.

After the 1991–92 season, Karl supposedly made a deal with Payton. If he would work hard on his outside shooting with Grgurich that summer, then Karl would give Gary what he wanted—a freer hand in running the Sonics' offense. Payton worked out and took from 500 to 1,000 jumpers per day. His offensive numbers improved to 13.5 points per game on 49.4 percent accuracy from the floor in 1992–93.

"Coach Grgurich is the one who helped me become the player I am today," Payton would say the following season. "I owe him everything. He stayed with me, gave me confidence."

In 1993–94, Payton enjoyed his finest season as a pro, registering career highs with 16.5 points, 2.9 steals, and 50.4 percent field-goal accuracy. He ranked second on the Sonics in scoring and seventh in the league in steals. Payton was named an All-Star and a member of the NBA All-Defensive Team for the first time. He scored a career-high 32 points against Charlotte, after coming up with a career-high eight steals against Golden State earlier in the season.

Finally, Payton was beginning to understand that he couldn't afford to play down to the level of his competition on the nights he was matched against mediocrities and still be considered among the best.

"I've got to start thinking, hey, no matter who it is, whether it is an elite point guard or not, I have got to play them all the same way," said Payton. "If I am not playing against an elite point guard, I slack up. That's my downfall."

When the Sonics reached the playoffs, there were huge expectations of success—the kind that generally accompany 63 regular-season victories. The first-round, best-of-five series was supposed to be a breeze against the eighth-seeded, under-.500, extremely young Denver Nuggets, but it was clear that Payton and the Sonics were very much on edge right from the start.

Gary had a nasty verbal sparring match with reporter Jim Moore of the *Seattle Post-Intelligencer* in reaction to a fairly innocuous question on the eve of the series. It was clear that the guy who makes the Sonics go was wound tighter than a drum before the opening jump in Game 1.

A 106-82 opening night rout of Denver at home did little to relax Payton and his keyed-up teammates. At halftime of the Sonics' 97–87 Game 2 victory, Payton nearly came to blows with teammate Ricky Pierce. According to Gary, Ricky had taken a second-quarter shot when the play that Payton wanted to run called for Pierce to pass the ball. After Pierce lost the ball, the two Sonics exchanged unpleasant words in the huddle, then before and during halftime.

Seattle Sonics coach George Karl sometimes clashed with the high-strung Payton, whose volatile personality often exploded at Karl and the other players.

"They got into a discussion at halftime," said Karl. "And they were threatening to get guns . . . The players told me they had guns in their bags. It was 'I will kill your family.' It was crazy."

"It was no big deal," claimed Payton.

After a particularly low-impact performance in a series-turning 110–93 Game 3 loss to the Nuggets at McNichols Arena, Payton returned to the locker room screaming like a madman.

According to Gary, "I said, 'This is garbage the way we came out and played.' Everybody is looking at me like, 'Damn, why is he going off?' I was going off because I saw the way we were playing and that we were going to get beat . . . We had no chemistry."

"He went crazy after the game," Karl said. "And everything he was saying . . . was a projection. He was yelling at himself. He was standing up there saying, 'We did this' and 'You are a so-and-so.' He's yelling at the team, but he's yelling at himself. He was saying, 'You guys dogged it. We let them kick our butts. We didn't come mentally ready.' And the other players were saying, 'Come on, you were the worst one out there.'"

Game 4 slipped away when the Sonics failed to score a field goal for the final 1:22 of regulation and the first 4:30 of the overtime period as Denver gained a series-tying, momentum-building 94–85 victory.

Again, Payton exploded in the locker room after the game, nearly fighting with Karl and Sam Perkins.

"Players and coaches don't do this," said Karl, reflecting on the incident. "I've fought players before, but those were guys who should be fought—not your best player. You never take on your best player."

And your best player, your invaluable court leader and the tone setter for an allegedly elite team, isn't supposed to be picking post-defeat fights in his own locker room just because he is frustrated. The Sonics were tight, and none of them seemed more wired for failure than Payton.

It mattered little that the final Game 5 was in Seattle, where the Sonics had won 37 of 41 regular-season home games. The Nuggets scrambled to a seven-point lead with three minutes left. In the final seconds, series standout Dikembe Mutombo blocked Payton's attempt at a game-tying shot, but Kendall Gill put back in the rebound to force an overtime. The Sonics should have had the momentum but played without poise or energy and lost, 98–84.

Karl, not usually one to refrain from directly criticizing his players, diplomatically attempted to excuse Payton's poor late performance by pointing out that his point guard was less than 100 percent physically because he had hurt his right foot in the first quarter when he landed awkwardly following the release of a jump shot.

Payton wasn't the only one feeling the pain in Seattle. The fans felt cheated. The media questioned whether the Sonics would ever win a thing with such a void in leadership. As Payton himself later admitted, the defeat was more accurately a measure of character than talent.

"Even when Game 5 went into overtime, I wasn't confident we were going to win," he said. "We were scared. All of us. I felt the same way."

5

A NEW ATTITUDE

Gary Payton went into the summer following the 1993–94 season still smarting from the Sonics' early playoff dismissal and disturbed by the way he and his team were now perceived. In the eyes of many, the Sonics were choke artists and Gary had been exposed as their unreliable floor leader. The pressure had transformed him into a tightly wound emotional volcano.

In time, Payton came to regret his feud with teammate Ricky Pierce, his too-frequent pouts, and his decision to skip the season-ending team meeting called by coach George Karl. His vast attitude adjustment was brought about in part by a conversation with Tim Grgurich during which Payton asked for frank input.

"I thought about it [the loss to Denver] every day for a month and a half, what I could have or should have done," said Gary. "And I realized

Payton attempts to recover the ball and Sonics forward Shawn Kemp looks on as Utah Jazz forwards Byron Russel, right, and Karl Malone, left, encroach during a May 28, 1996, game in Seattle.

if I had stood up and taken a little more responsibility last season, we probably wouldn't have lost to Denver."

Payton also realized that his infighting with Karl had to stop, in the interests of fulfilling his role as the Sonics' leader.

"Coach Grgurich told me, 'You have all the tools, go ahead and do it. Don't start problems.' He said if coach Karl takes you out of a game, you can't give him a problem, because everybody else sees it and says, 'Gary talks that way. I can, too.' . . . At first, I wouldn't accept it because of my personality and ego. Then I realized Gary had to change. I had to go in with a new attitude, so it [another playoff embarrassment] would not happen again."

Remarkably, midway through 1994–95, Payton even joined Shawn Kemp and Nate McMillan in calling for a critical clear-the-air meeting with the coach that helped to settle a dispute between Karl and Kendall Gill. Off the court, Payton was playing the role of peacemaker instead of peacebreaker. On the court, he was better than ever.

The Sonics won 57 games behind Payton and his best effort in five years as a pro. Payton established career highs with 33-point games on two occasions. He set the club record for consecutive field goals made by going 14 for 14 from the floor in a 32-point effort against Cleveland, joining Wilt Chamberlain, Bailey Howell, and Billy McKinney as the only NBA players to have a perfect shooting game with a minimum of 14 attempts. Payton made 15 of 17 shots from the field in a 32-point, seven-assist game against Portland. He enjoyed his second straight All-Star nod and was runner-up to Sacramento's Mitch Richmond in the voting for the game's Most

Valuable Player after registering 15 assists in 23 minutes.

Overall, Gary averaged 20.6 points per game, 7.1 assists, and 2.49 steals. Payton's .509 field accuracy was fifth-best among NBA guards and his free-throw shooting soared from an unacceptable .595 showing in 1993–94 to a respectable .716 in 1994-95 and .748 in 1995–96.

Payton seemed to be growing up, at last. He cited the mellowing effects of raising his two children, Raquel, 6, and Gary Jr., 2, with his fiancé, Monique, a former junior college women's basketball player.

"Once you become a father, you have to grow up, just like they are growing up," said Payton, "I don't want my kids' friends talking about how their father is acting like a crazy clown on the court."

Though Gary's growth as a player and a man helped his game, Payton broke a finger on his left hand in the last week of the regular season and then played with the injury during the first-round postseason series against the Los Angeles Lakers. He shot only 47.8 percent from the floor, and he managed only 21 assists and five steals in the four games that the Lakers needed to send the Sonics home.

All Payton could do was assume his share of the blame again. He began the 1995–96 campaign determined to make Seattle a genuine title con-tender. He was willing to do anything to erase the perceptions that he and his teammates were incapable of sustaining their excellence under the heat of playoff pressure.

In 1995–96, the Sonics cruised to 64 regular-season wins as Payton averaged 19.3 points, 7.5 assists, and 2.85 steals. He rang up 18 points, five rebounds, and five assists in the All-Star Game.

"You could argue that he is the best point guard in the league," said Houston Rockets coach Rudy Tomjanovich.

"I am directing this team a little better than I have the last two or three years. I'm more serious. I'm more productive," said Payton.

Payton recorded his fourth career triple-double against the Los Angeles Clippers on March 18, rang up a career-high 38 points against the Sacramento Kings—and matched his career high with 11 rebounds on March 24. Gary notched a career-high 17 assists against the Charlotte Hornets on March 27.

According to Payton, the best way to contain him was to put a bigger guard on him, making it more difficult for him to go down low and to do his penetration-and-pass dissection job on the defense. Payton made teams pay for letting him take open jumpers from long distance.

"I don't think there will be many teams who want me to continue shooting the jumper, because I am going to stick it," said Payton.

On May 6, a delighted Payton was named the NBA's Defensive Player of the Year. He won the honor convincingly, amassing 56 votes out of a possible 113. It marked the first time that a Sonic had won the award and the first time a center had not won the award since 1990–91. Certainly, the quick hands and feet that Gary used to average his 2.85 steals per game went a long way toward explaining why the Sonics' opponents compiled the second-lowest field-goal percentage in the league at .438.

"We've got a defensive-oriented team and we had a great year," said Karl. "And Gary is the

Payton's path to the basket is blocked by the body of the Chicago Bulls' Luc Longley during a January 6, 1995, game in Chicago. The SuperSonics defeated the Bulls 108–101.

leader of that defense. We rely upon a great deal of pressure and rotation for our success. But he can also defend the ball. I think everyone knows he is very, very important for our team."

"I think I have got great hands," said Payton. "And the style coach has let us play is the reason I am getting better and better each year . . . He lets me make mistakes, because he knows I am going to come back and try to get a big play or a big steal. I work so hard at it.

"One of my best tactics is to overplay my man and force him in another direction. I fake like I am going the other way, then I make my move and suddenly the ball is in my hands, not his, and he's going, 'What happened?' I live for that. When I force the other coach to have his two-guard [shooting guard] bring the ball up [instead of his point], I know I have won the battle."

Awards were nice, but playoff success was the only thing that would provide Payton and his Sonics a chance to cleanse their reputations.

"All we seemed to care about going into the playoffs was getting past the first round, which everyone knows we couldn't do for the previous two years," said Payton, looking back. "All we wanted to do was show the world we weren't chokers. I don't think there will ever be such a great team that will struggle in the first round of the playoffs like we did."

It didn't help the Sonics' confidence when Shawn Kemp earned a one-game postseason suspension in the team's regular-season finale and was forced to watch Game 1 of the opening series against Sacramento.

Fortunately for Seattle, Payton was in high gear and compensated for the loss of the All-Star center. Payton racked up 29 points, 9 assists, 6 rebounds, and 4 steals in a 97–85 win. The performance had Karl singing his praises.

"Gary had big shoulders for us," said the appreciative coach. "We rode him all night long."

Payton had only 10 points and 7 assists in Game 2, and Sacramento won 90–81, evening the best-of-five series and causing panic in Seattle.

"Talk about scary . . . When we lost the second game at home, it was like, 'Here we go again,'" said Payton. "The media was bringing up the past. But coach Karl yelled, 'Let's shut up these guys forever and the only way to do it is to win!' We just put our foot down and did the job."

Next up for Seattle were the Houston Rockets, smarting from having lost nine straight meetings with the Sonics. During the season series, a four-game sweep, Payton was the chief Rocket killer, averaging 28.8 points per game.

Game 1 in Seattle set the tone for the Western Conference semifinal series as the Sonics cruised, 108–75. Payton nailed four early three-point jumpers and finished with 28 points and 7 assists. He also spearheaded the defensive pressure on Houston that kept the ball out of the hands of Hakeem Olajuwon, who had only nine shots and a career playoff low of six points.

In a 105–101 Game 2 Seattle win, Payton had 18 points, 5 rebounds, 5 assists, and a key strip of Olajuwon with 10.1 seconds left and the Sonics leading by only two points. Payton went for 28 points, including two free throws with 10 seconds left that gave Seattle its 115–112 victory margin, in Game 3. Led by Payton's 24 points and 11 assists, the Sonics went into overtime to sweep the defending champions in Game 4.

By that time, Houston coach Rudy Tomjanovich had his fill of Payton. "He is just the key

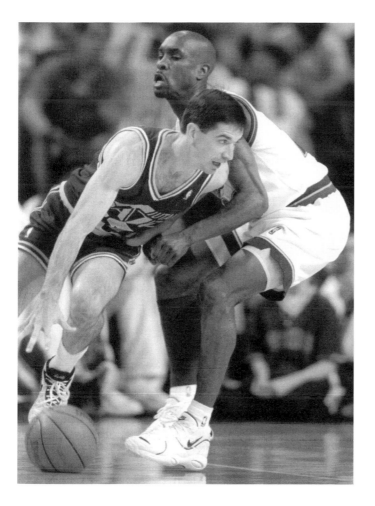

The Utah Jazz's John Stockton drives around Gary Payton in the first quarter of the Western Conference Finals game seven, June 2, 1996, in Seattle. Though Payton considered Stockton the toughest NBA player to guard, the Sonics beat the Jazz, 90–86.

to everything they do, that is all. He is the engine behind their offense with the way he penetrates and pushes the ball on the break."

Payton was ready to go head-to-head in the Western Finals against his hero, the Utah Jazz's veteran playmaker John Stockton.

"I think he is the best," said the 27-year-old Payton of Stockton, the 34-year-old NBA all-time leader in assists and steals. "I love his game so much I want to be just like him . . . because he does everything I do but with more savvy, intelligence, and control . . . He has been through the wars. He doesn't have a weakness."

That was not the way it looked in Game 1, when Payton ran rings around Stockton, who was still nursing a strained hamstring from the previous series. Payton held Stockton to 4 points and 7 assists while ringing up 21 points, 7 assists, 4 rebounds, and 3 steals of his own.

Through five games, Payton was dynamic. However, in Game 6, Payton was invisible (10 points, 7 assists, and 5 turnovers) and Utah won to force a final game.

The doomsayers were pointing to the Sonics' vulnerability against a poised, veteran, Jazz team. And again Payton's mettle would be going under the microscope in Game 7. This time he elevated his game to the occasion, amassing 21 points, 6 rebounds, and 5 assists as the Sonics took the final step to the Finals with a 90–86 victory.

"I can't imagine a better point guard for our style," said Karl. "There are some great point

(From left) Seattle Super-Sonics coach George Karl celebrates with assistant coach Tim Grgurich and trainer Frank Furtado after the Sonics' 101–87 victory over the Sacramento Kings on May 2, 1996, in the first round of the NBA playoffs.

guards in the league, but there is not one I would rather have playing for me than Gary Payton.

"He's not a great shooter. He's not really quick. He's not a great jumper. He's not a great ball-handler. But the thing is, he's a great winner. Stockton is a better playmaker and there are better shooters and so on. But the total package, what he brings defensively and all his other assets, makes him the best."

Now it was time to make a stand against the Chicago Bulls, against whom the Sonics had split two games during the regular season, winning the meeting in Seattle in large part because of Payton's strip of Jordan in the final seconds. Payton had earned Jordan's respect.

"His game is spontaneous on the defensive end," said Jordan. "He's a good court leader offensively, too. He is a point guard who makes things happen on both ends."

But Chicago stopped Seattle in Game 6 and the NBA Championship once again eluded Gary Payton and the Sonics.

"The Bulls knew how to get the calls," said Payton. "They knew how to act. They knew how to stop our runs. We're still learning. I am going to sit down this summer, look at the film of this series, and say, 'What could I have done differently? What could I improve on?' This was a learning experience for us . . .We just have to look at this and say this isn't an ending period for us. We are not going to die after this. We just have to take this as a lesson, learn from this and try to come back."

6

GROWING UP

In addition to his reputation for mouthing off, Gary Payton had built a record of endurance. In his four years at Oregon State, he had started every game. In the NBA, he had played in 354 consecutive games until a league suspension sat him down on March 15, 1996.

"My father always used to tell me, 'If you can play, play. Be tough.'"

"Gary is one of those guys who gets stronger in the second half," said George Karl. "I think everybody gets tired, but he gets stronger through everybody else getting tired. There are certain players who are like that. Moses Malone was like that. Michael [Jordan] is like that. You might be able to beat them early in the game, but defensively they don't ever drop. They stay there and when you get tired, they control you."

Gary Payton keeps a tight defense on rookie Matt Maloney of the Houston Rockets during a May 15, 1997, game in Seattle, but the Sonics lost to Houston in the playoffs.

Gradually Payton gained more control over his behavior. With some hesitation, U.S. Olympic coach Lenny Wilkens picked him to replace the injured Glenn Robinson on the 1996 Olympic Dream Team. Wilkens was concerned about Gary's embarrassing the Americans with his conduct on the court before a worldwide audience. But Payton's hands and feet did all the talking as the U.S. romped to a gold medal.

A free agent that summer, Payton had offers from five other teams before signing a seven-year, $89.5 million deal to remain in Seattle.

"I want to play for one organization," he said. "I am having my jersey retired at Oregon State and someday I would like that to happen here . . . To win a championship for this organization and these fans—there would be nothing better."

His improving relationship with coach Karl was another factor in his re-signing with Seattle. "We got tight and he started to get more confidence in me and gave me more leeway with the team, more plays, more responsibility," said Payton. "Once he did that, I felt I had to give something back to him by being productive and respectful. I began going up to him and telling him things that were on my mind."

Karl told him, "You can lead badly or you can lead the right way."

But Payton was not entirely subdued. "I can't let that go," he said. "I can try to change a lot of things, but I can't change that. That is what keeps the fire in me. That is what energizes me. Like my father says, 'That is your game. That is you. You can control it, but don't lose it.'"

Once again the 1996–97 SuperSonics looked like a championship team until the time came to play for the title. Their critics called them chokers. They romped to the 1997 Pacific Division title with a 57–25 record, then went into a funk against the Phoenix Suns, losing two of the first three games in the opening playoff round. Rex Chapman led the Suns to a Game 1 106–101 win with 42 points. Payton and company didn't stop Chapman until the final game.

As they had done in '96 against Sacramento, Seattle avoided early elimination by rallying to take the last two games. It wasn't easy. In Game 4 a Phoenix three-pointer tied the game with under two seconds to play, forcing the Sonics to go overtime for a 122–115 win. In the showdown game, they frittered away a 22-point lead before regrouping for the 116–92 clincher.

For all their talent, the Sonics seemed to lack what it took to make a champion a champion.

They continued to make it hard for themselves, confirming the doubts of their critics as they lost three of the first four games in the next round against the Houston Rockets. Houston had added Charles Barkley since the Sonics swept them the year before. Barkley teamed with veterans Hakeem Olajuwon and Clyde Drexler to form a formidable lineup, but it was a rookie, Matt Maloney, whose three-pointers tormented the Sonics.

In Game 1 on May 5, the Rockets' three-pointers sank the Sonics, 112–102. Two days later, Seattle built a big halftime lead, saw it whittled away, but held on to tie the best-of-seven set, 106–101.

Then they lost two in a row, the second at home when Maloney scored eight three-pointers in an overtime 110–106 win. The Rockets went home to finish them off, but the Sonics, in what had become an annual pattern, made a dogfight of it to the final buzzer. Coach George Karl switched Gary Payton to guard the red-hot Maloney, and Payton held the rookie pointless on six three-point attempts while scoring 21 in a 100–94 win.

Back home for Game 6, Payton's 19 points, 13 assists, and 5 steals helped the Sonics build up a 22-point lead, but again they made an easy win difficult. The Rockets closed the gap to 2 points with 31 seconds left before Payton's spinning lefthand hook clinched the 99–96 victory.

Game 7 seemed to reflect the Sonics' perennial game-time split personality. They fought the

The Houston Rockets' Charles Barkley has the ball but is surrounded by SuperSonics Sam Perkins (left) and Gary Payton (right) during the third quarter of a Western Conference semifinal game May 13, 1997, in Houston.

Rockets even in the first half, turned cold in the second half, furiously closed a 14-point deficit to 2 in the final four minutes, but failed to score on their final possession. Though the Sonics closed to within 2 in the final minute, their season ended early again with a 96–91 defeat.

As usual, Gary Payton did not go quietly, on or off the court. He blamed the loss on bad luck, but Houston had outplayed them at their own defensive game.

Payton also second-guessed his coach. "I think we should have [switched to the smaller lineup] earlier in the game. It was a coaching decision."

Seattle traded Shawn Kemp to Cleveland before the 1997–98 season but kept on winning. The Sonics and Los Angeles Lakers fought for first place in the West. Payton was among the leaders in points, assists, and steals, and led all Western Conference guards in the NBA All-Star balloting.

There was one difference: they lost a game to the Minnesota Timberwolves. After an NBA-record 26-game losing streak over six seasons to Seattle, the Timberwolves won one, 112–103.

But the Sonics had long ago proven they could win the conference with ease. They were determined that their string of postseason failures would not end the way almost every year of Payton's career had ended so far: watching the NBA Finals at home on television.

Acknowledged as the best defensive point guard in the league, Gary Payton still had to prove that he had what it takes to be a champion.

CHRONOLOGY

1968   Born in Oakland, California

1985   Teams with Greg Foster to lead Skyline High School
to Northern California championship game as a junior

1986   Accepts scholarship to play basketball at Oregon
State University (OSU)

1987   Earns the nickname "The Glove" as he is named Pac-10
Defensive Player of the Year and Pac-10 Rookie of the
Year and sets school single-season record for assists
with 229

1989   Becomes OSU's all-time assist man and leads team
in scoring (21.8), assists (8.1), and steals (3.0)

1990   Earns *Sports Illustrated* College Player of the Year and
Pac-10 Player of the Year honors; Drafted No. 2 overall
by Seattle in NBA draft

1994   Chosen an All-Star for the first time

1996   Named NBA Defensive Player of the Year; wins gold medal
as late addition to the U.S. Olympic Team; signs seven-year
$89.5-million deal to remain in Seattle

STATISTICS

GARY PAYTON

NBA Regular Season

Season/Team	G	MIN	FG PCT	3-Pt PCT	FT PCT	AST	STL	PTS	Averages APG	PPG
90-91 Seattle	82	2244	.450	.077	.711	528	165	588	6.4	7.2
91-92 Seattle	81	2549	.451	.130	.669	506	147	764	6.2	9.4
92-93 Seattle	82	2548	.494	.206	.770	399	177	1110	4.9	13.5
93-94 Seattle	82	2881	.504	.278	.595	494	188	1349	6.0	16.5
94-95 Seattle	82	3015	.504	.302	.716	583	204	1689	7.1	20.6
95-96 Seattle	81	3162	.484	.328	.748	608	231	1563	7.5	19.3
96-97 Seattle	82	3213	.476	.313	.715	583	197	1785	7.1	21.8
TOTALS	572	19612	.486	.302	.704	3701	1309	8848	6.5	15.5

NBA Playoffs

Season/Team	G	MIN	FG PCT	3-Pt PCT	FT PCT	AST	STL	PTS	Averages APG	PPG
90-91 Seattle	5	135	.407	.000	1.000	32	8	24	6.4	4.8
91-92 Seattle	8	221	.466	.000	.583	38	8	61	4.8	7.6
92-93 Seattle	19	605	.443	.167	.676	70	34	234	3.7	12.3
93-94 Seattle	5	181	.493	.333	.421	28	8	79	5.6	15.8
94-95 Seattle	4	172	.478	.200	.417	21	5	71	5.3	17.8
95-96 Seattle	21	911	.485	.410	.633	143	37	434	6.8	20.7
96-97 Seattle	12	546	.412	.333	.820	104	26	285	8.7	23.8
TOTALS	74	2771	.454	.355	.659	436	126	1188	5.9	16.1

G	games	AST	assists
MIN	minutes	STL	steals
FG PCT	field goal percentage	PTS	points
3-Pt PCT	3-point percentage	APG	assists per game
FT PCT	free throw percentage	PPG	points per game

FURTHER READING

Karl, George. *This Game's the Best*. New York: St. Martin's Press,1997.

Gutman, Bill. *Michael Jordan*. Brookfield, CT: The Millbrook Press, Inc., 1995.

Peterson, Tom. *Seattle Supersonics*. Mankato, MN: Creative Education Inc., 1989.

Sampson, Curt. *Full Court Pressure: A Tumultuous Season with Coach Karl and the Seattle Sonics*. New York: Doubleday, 1995.

Vancil, Mark. *NBA Basketball*. San Francisco: Collins Publishers, 1995.

ABOUT THE AUTHOR

Howard Blatt is a former pro basketball beat writer for the *New York Daily News*, and the author of young adult pro basketball books *Magic: Against the Odds* and *Dream Team III: Quest for the Gold*.

INDEX

PHOTO CREDITS

AP/Wide World Photos: pp. 2, 8, 13, 15, 23, 26, 30, 34, 37, 38, 41, 44, 48, 51, 52, 54, 58, 60; Oregon State University: p. 18.